Presented by
**MILAN MATRA**

# 4

BOTATA
ボタタッ
BOTA (PLIP)
ボタッ
...WHY... IS... SITRI...?

GAKU (SLUMP)
ガクッ
GUH... UH...
TOBARI! HANG IN THERE!
21st Demon:
The Director's Office
KIIIIN (VWEEEEE)
キィイイン
HEH-HEH-HEH... NAUGHTY, NAUGHTY, "BLUE ARROW MARQUIS" LERAJE.
YOU MUSTN'T DEFY THE "RING OF SOLOMON."

...ARE YOU REALLY SITRI?
LONG TIME NO SEE, "PRINCE OF FEAR ASTAROTH."

IT HURT A WHOLE LOT GETTING STABBED IN THE CHEST BY YOU......
ギロ
GIRO (GLARE)

WHAT'S GOING ON? I COULD'VE SWORN I KILLED HER...

IS THIS HARUOMI ......? NO—
IS THIS THE WORK OF THE RING OF SOLOMON?

HFF.
HFFF.
......WHAT'S YOUR NAME?

... LERAJ—
NO.

YOUR "BRANCH" ...
YOUR NAME AS A "WATCHER EGG."

TOBARI KEMIZUKA...

.........
I'M SORRY, TOBARI.

YOUR LIFE WILL VANISH SOON.
YOUR LIFE AS A PERSON WILL END.

I KNOW THIS IS SELFISH OF ME TO SAY, BUT......
...I'M SORRY I CAN'T SAVE YOU.

GH!

WHAT ARE YOU TALKING ABOUT ......!?
UNBE-LIEV-ABLE.

......BEING APOLOGIZED TO BY THE VERY PERSON WHO KILLED ME...
...I DON'T EVEN KNOW HOW TO RESPOND...

YOU REALLY ARE......
...NO... FAIR...

GAKU (LURCH)
GUH... UH......
TOBARI !?
...GET OUT, EVELINA...
GOPO (HACK)
HE'S... THE "BRANCH'S" ...
TOBARI! TOBARI !?
~~~!!
~~~

... YOU—
DON'T TALK TO ME.

WE SHOULD GO.
TOBARI SAID TO.

......
"DUKE OF CRUELTY."

LATELY, THE "BRANCHES" ARE BEING MENTALLY ALTERED TO KEEP THEM FROM DEFECTING OR SNEAKING AWAY.
THE GOAL BEING TO REDUCE ALL RISK OF THEM BETRAYING "GOETIA," NO MATTER HOW SMALL.

WHAT DID YOU GUYS SEE IN GOETIA?

CHEAP TRICKS WON'T WORK ON ME. I'M FREE.
IF YOU CLAIM TO BE THE SAME, THEN LIVE FREE—FOR HER SAKE TOO.

IF YOU STILL INSIST ON STANDING IN OUR WAY AFTER THAT...
...THEN LET'S REALLY HAVE A FIGHT TO THE DEATH.
LET'S GO, ZILCH. DAD AND THE OTHERS WILL BE WORRIED.
......
RIGHT.

...HEY, HARUOMI IO. YOU KILLED ME WITHOUT ASKING MY NAME OR EVEN OFFERING AN APOLOGY...
THAT'S BECAUSE YOU'D KILLED ALL THOSE INNOCENT PEOPLE.

HMMM... TRUE.
OH WELL...
NWAAA-AAAH!?
HISHI (CLAMP)
THANKS TO THAT, I GET TO BE WITH YOU LIKE THIS WHENEVER I WANT.

......

...FINE. WHAT'S YOUR NAME?
AND PUT SOME PROPER CLOTHES ON.
HUH...? GETTING HUGGED BY A NAKED GIRL DOESN'T MAKE YOU HAPPY ...?
GYUUU (SQUEEZE)
GR-RRRR!

MY NAME IS......
SAAAA (SSSHH)
サァァァ
I FORGOT.
MORE IMPORTANTLY... THE POWER OF THE RING.
SHUUUU (SSSHHH)
シュウウウ
I THINK YOU ALREADY KNOW THIS, BUT SHE'S COMING INSIDE YOU ......
!
......YEAH. I KNOW.
INSIDE ME...
THE POWER OF THE RING, HUH...?
WILL I APPEAR INSIDE HIM SOMEDAY TOO...?

HATO. TELL US WHERE MUROHIME, MY DAD, AND THE OTHERS ARE RIGHT NOW.

Hold on. I'm guiding them to the control room as we speak!

MASTER.
HM?

...WAS IT RIGHT FOR US TO GET OUT AHEAD OF THE OTHERS?

...PROB-ABLY NOT.
BUT THEY WENT TO END THINGS ONCE AND FOR ALL.

HIS GUILT AND SENSE OF DUTY COMPEL HIM.
AND THEY LET US ESCAPE FIRST SO WE WOULDN'T GET INVOLVED. WE HAVE TOO MUCH PRECIOUS DATA.
THAT'S ABSURD OF THEM......
...BUT I DON'T HATE THEM FOR IT.
...INDEED.

DA
DA
DA (TMP)
IO-KUN IS CERTAINLY GOING TO BE MAD AT US FOR THIS.
YOU'RE RIGHT.
I'VE ALWAYS BEEN A VERY...... SELFISH FATHER.
DOKA (BASH)
GWAH!
JA (CHAK)
FREEZE!!

BA (BAH)
SU (SWF)
YOU'RE NOT GETTING AWAY.
!
BIKA (ZAP)
ZA (ZSH)
BIIII (BZZZZT)
JI (FZZT)

DOKAA (BOOM)
KUH!

GOOOOO (WOOOO)
......I ALMOST GOT A STAR-SHAPED BURN.

OOOO
IT'S OKAY. I CAN CUT OFF ALL SEQUENCES.
I'LL REDUCE YOUR HUMAN BODY TO DUST.

NO THANK YOU.

KIIII (VWEEEEE)
NO NEED TO HOLD BACK FOR ME!
BABIN (ZAP)
SHUN (SHWIP)
WHAT—?
BAKI (CRUNCH)

UWAH!
AACK!!
DOKA (BASH)

MURO-HIME-KUN!
DO (BLAST)
DO
ARE YOU ALL RIGHT, PROFES-SOR!?
DO
DO

YEAH, BUT THE SECURITY AROUND THE CONTROL ROOM IS TIGHT.
WE'LL HAVE TO GO ABOUT THIS THE OTHER WAY.
WHAT OTHER WAY?
GASHA (CLATTER)

THE TOP DIREC-TOR'S OFFICE.
WE SHOULD BE ABLE TO OPERATE IT FROM THERE.

THE DIRECTOR'S OFFICE, MITSUKURI-SAN!
Hold on. I'm scanning for it now.
ZA (ZSH)

...OKAY. IT LOOKS LIKE THE CIRCUITS ARE CON-NECTED.
AND IT'S NOT FAR FROM THERE.
KATA (CLACK)
KATA

BUT SOME-THING'S ODD HERE...
PROFESSOR IO, DON'T TRY TO DO THE IMPOSSIBLE. GET BACK HERE!

PRO-FESSOR LEVI SAYS NOT TO OVERDO IT AND TO COME BACK ...
......

...PRO-FESSOR.
I WON'T LET YOU THROW YOUR LIFE AWAY JUST SO YOU CAN TAKE RESPONSIBILITY.

HA-HA-HA. I'M NOT THAT BRAVE.

THAT'S RIGHT.
IF ONLY I'D HAD THAT COURAGE BACK THEN—

WHAT ON EARTH...
...HAP-PENED HERE...?

I THOUGHT IT WAS ODD THAT WE WEREN'T MEETING ANY RESISTANCE, BUT...
YEAH...

... ANYWAY, LET'S SET THE DETONA-TION!
ZA (ZSH)

GOBAA (BLORP)

DON (BAM)
I'LL TAKE CARE OF HER!!
SO HURRY, PROFES-SOR!!

RIGHT!
THANKS!
JUST BUY ME A LITTLE TIME!

IF WE CAN JUST JOIN UP WITH ZILCH-KUN, IT SHOULDN'T TAKE EVEN FIVE MINUTES TO GET OUT OF HERE.
PI (BEEP)
ピッ
PI
ピッ
BUT IF WE CAN'T, THEN MUROHIME-KUN AT LEAST HAS TO...
PI
ピッ

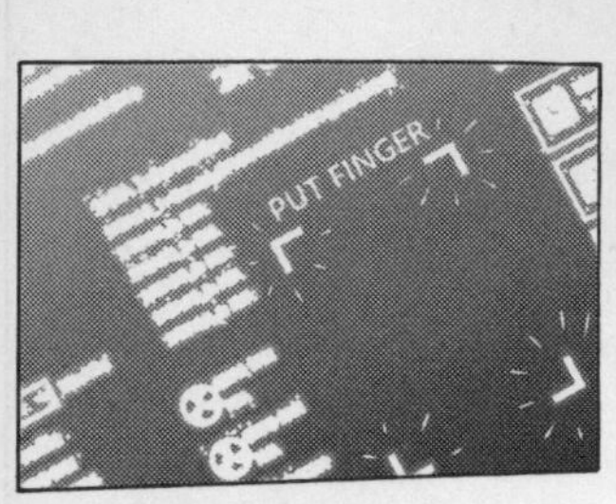
PUT FINGER

NOW FOR THE DIRECTOR'S FINGER-PRINT TO SCAN...

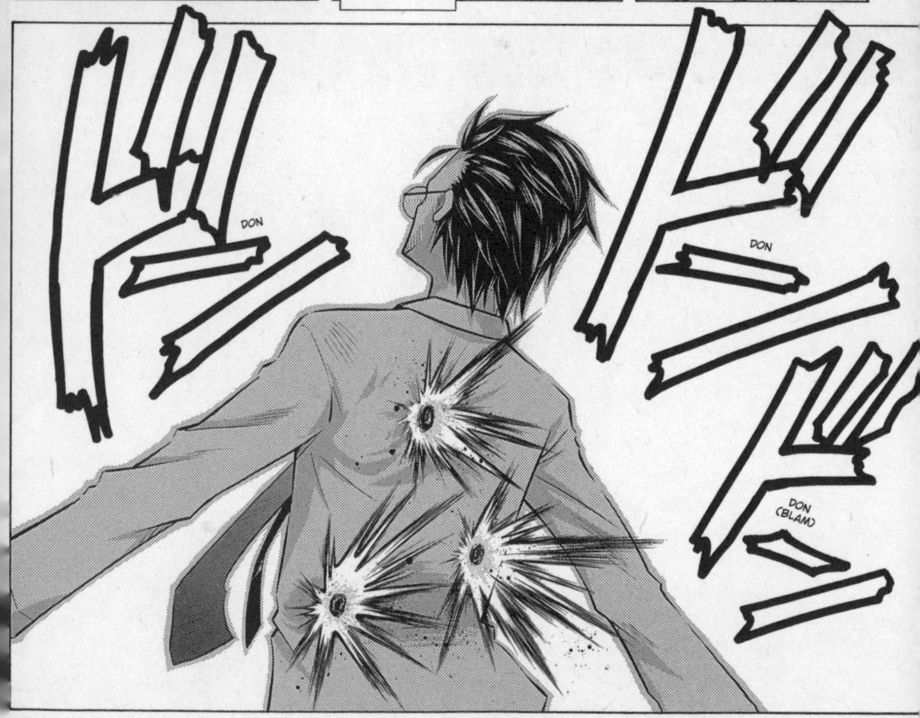
DON
DON
DON (BLAM)

22nd Demon: Atonement

GAH... HFF...
YORO (STAGGER)
BISHA (SPLAT)
GA (THUMP)
PRO-FES-SOR IO!
BA (WHIP)
DOSU (STAB)

SHE GOT M......
THIS IS UNBECOMING OF A KNIGHT, BUT...
... PARDON ME FOR STRIKING FROM BEHIND.
ZU (ZSH)
GOFF ...!
MURO... HIME-KUN...!

I NEVER THOUGHT IT'D COME TO THIS.

WHY DID YOU KILL THE DIRECTOR AND HIS MEN, PROFESSOR IO?
BUKIN (TING)
ARE YOU AS BARBARIC AS I'VE HEARD?
DON'T TAKE YOUR EYES OFF THE GIRL, "CIMERIES, CONQUEROR OF THE DARK CONTINENT."

OKAY.
NO... WE DIDN'T KILL THEM...!

ZUBYU (YANK)
KAH ...!

...AN ORDINARY HUMAN WOULD BE DEAD BY NOW.
YOU'RE PRETTY TOUGH.

WHAT MUROHIME-KUN SAID... IS TRUE... WE DIDN'T... DO ANYTHING.
IT'S THE RESULT OF INTERNAL STRIFE... AND WARRING FACTIONS... DON'T YOU SEE...?

OF ALL THE RIDICULOUS —
THAT MIGHT BE TRUE.
TSUI (SNUB)

I DON'T CARE ABOUT THE DIRECTOR.
BUT I KNOW WHAT YOU TWO ARE DOING.
YOU'RE TRYING TO BLOW THIS PLACE UP TO ERASE ALL EVIDENCE OF IT.

WHAT ......?
SO THAT'S THEIR AIM.
CHA (K-CLICK)
THAT'D BE TROUBLE FOR US.

ACTU-
ALLY...
ZUPA
(SLASH)
...IT'S
NO
TROUBLE
AT ALL.

GIVEN WHERE THIS BUILDING STANDS, OF COURSE YOU'RE GOING TO BE STORMED BY THE ENEMY.
YOU ...!
FOOL.
IMPOSSIBLE! YOU'RE SUPPOSED TO BE CONFINED TO THE 5TH ISOLATION LEVEL!
ZA (ZWOOSH)
I ONLY STAYED IN THERE BECAUSE I WAS A MITE SLEEPY.
ISOLATION? CONFINED?

A "BRANCH" THAT WOULD WARRANT BEING ISOLATED BY GOETIA? COULD THESE DEAD BODIES BE HER DOING...?
Muro-hime-san, what's going on over there!?
The security cameras in the director's office have been damaged, so I can't see a thing!
Profes... fzzzt... lo...... fzzt.
WHAT? I CAN'T HEAR YOU!
BACHI (ZAP)
ZUOOO (ZWOOOOP)
!!
OH NO...!!

HAAAH.
HAAAAH.
POOR HUMAN.
DO YOU HATE GOETIA?
...NO, I...
... HATE... MYSELF.
FOR NEVER STEPPING BACK AND REALIZING... HOW BARBARIC MY AMBITIONS WERE.
...THIS IS MY ATONEMENT...
I WILL ACCEPT IT.
...I'LL SEE TO THAT.

ATTENTION "BRANCHES" AND ALL PERSONNEL!
I AM HELLENTZA FITZENGAHEN.
THE NEW KING.
WHA...!?
THIS FACILITY WILL BE WIPED OUT SHORTLY WITHOUT A TRACE!!
THOSE WHO WISH TO FOLLOW IN MY FOOT-STEPS, GO TO THE 5TH ISOLATION LEVEL.
...BUT THOSE WHO LACK FAITH AND CLING TO LIFE, I SHALL FACE ANNIHI-LATION.
YOU'RE TRYING TO TAKE OVER GOETIA!?
CHA (K-CLICK)
チャッ
YOU'RE SERIOUS ABOUT DESTROY-ING THIS PLACE!? NOT SO FAST!

GOGA (BOOM)
KIN (TING)
SHUN (SHWIP)

ゴオオオオ
GOOOOO (WOOOO)
I WILL FOLLOW MY KING.
A MOST WISE DECISION.
SU ス (SWF)

...... WHAT'S THE MATTER? THE BYPASS IS STILL ACTIVE, YOU KNOW?

HAAAH. HAAAH...
KUH ...!

GO ゴ (RUMBLE)
GO ゴ
GO ゴ
PRO-FESSOR IO, NO...! LET'S CALL THIS OFF...!

MUROHIME-KUN...I'M SORRY FOR PROPOSING SOMETHING SO SELFISH, BUT...
YORO ヨロ... (SWAY)
...GO ON... ESCAPE WITHOUT ME...

THANKS FOR ALL YOU'VE DONE.
PLEASE TAKE CARE... OF MY SON...
WH-WHAT ARE YOU SAYING ...?

PRO-FES-SOR!
HEL-LENTZA-KUN... WAS IT...?
RELEASE ...
...THE "EGG" CHIL-DREN...
...I WON'T MISTREAT MY SIBLINGS.
スル
ZURU (DRAG)
PI (BEEP)
MARIE. AYANA. NOW I'LL ALSO—
WHAT ARE YOU DOING, DAD!!!?

ゴォォォォォ
GOOOOO (WOOOO)
WHAT THE HELL ARE YOU DOING ...!?

オオオオ
OOOO (VOOOO)
HARU ...
... OMI...

I CAN'T BELIEVE... SHE GOT OUT.

YOU WENT... AND DID SOMETHING CRAZY AGAIN.
I'M...FINE. IT'S YOUR FATHER WHO NEEDS ...!
WHY WOULD BOTH MURO-HIME AND MY DAD...
...BE WILLING TO GO SO FAR FOR THIS ......?
SO THAT'S THE KID .........
DO IT, AMON.
HUH?
DO IT.
GIN (GLARE)
BIKUU (JUMP)
E-EEEEE!

GOUN (FWOOSH)

SHUPAA (ZWOOSH)
KUH ...
BON (FWOOSH)
SHIT!
GU (GRIP)
KIIIIIN (TIIIING)
!
GOETIA IS FOOLISH.
THINKING THEY, PETTY HUMANS, COULD CONTROL DEMONS WITHOUT PAYING A PRICE OR EVEN OFFERING A SACRIFICE.
ZA (ZSH)

GUH ... AH...
KIIII (VWEEEE)
キイイイ
I-I CAN'T... MO...VE.
ZI... LCH.
WHAT'S THIS PRES-SURE...?
EVEN IF IT WAS TRIGGERED BY GOD...
ZURU (DRAG)
ずる...
UUGH......

...IT TRULY IS THE EPITOME OF IMBECILIC FOLLY.

BISHI (JAB)
BUT THAT MAN...

...IS WHAT BECOMES OF UNDER-STANDING, DELIBERA-TION, AND DETERMI-NATION.
I HOLD NO INTEREST IN SUCH A LIFE, BUT...

...IF YOU ARE HUMAN ...
...AS WELL AS HIS CHILD, THEN WATCH WHAT BECOMES OF HIM.

...HONESTLY, WHAT ARE YOU DOING ...?
THIS ISN'T... FUNNY...
DAD!!
...HARUOMI. THE TEN YEARS I LIVED WITH YOU... REALLY WERE... PEACEFUL.
BUT I...LET COUNT-LESS... CHILDREN DIE...
NO...... I KILLED THEM.
ゴオォォォ
GOOOOOOO (WOOOOOO)
I NEED TO PAY... FOR WHAT I DID...
I NEED TO ATONE FOR MY SINS ......

...AND... FOR WHAT I DID TO YOU TOO...

WE... MADE YOU BEAR...
...A HEAVY CROSS...

...YEAH, IT REALLY IS HEAVY...

BUT! I'M NOT AS HELP-LESS AS I USED TO BE!
I'M NOT POWERLESS LIKE I WAS BACK THEN, WHEN I LOST MY LITTLE SISTER AND FRIEND WITHOUT BEING ABLE TO DO A THING!
I'VE GAINED THE STRENGTH TO SAVE JUST ABOUT ANYONE!!

IT MAY NOT HAVE BEEN THE RIGHT WAY TO GO ABOUT IT...

...I'M GONNA USE THIS STRENGTH THE RIGHT WAY SO I DON'T CHANGE PEOPLE'S LIVES FOR THE WORSE!!

...AND I COULD HURT SOMEBODY IF I MISUSE IT, BUT...

SO QUIT SAYING EVERY-THING...
...IS YOUR FAULT!!

MARIE. OUR SON IS DIFFERENT THAN US. HE GREW UP RIGHT...
THANKS... HARUOMI.

ZU (ZSH)
GUH... UH...
DAD!?
BA (BAH)

I'M GONNA HELP YOU, SO DON'T MOVE ...!
STAY BACK... I'M OUT OF TIME...

—THIRTY MORE SECONDS.

BELIEVE IN YOUR-SELF...
...HARU-OMI.

I WANT YOU TO SAVE...
...AS MANY "BRANCH" CHILDREN AS YOU CAN.

I'M COUNTING ON YOU.
ガク
GAKUN (LURCH)
!
HARUOMI!!

DOOOOOO (BOOOOOOOM)
23rd Demon: "Lord of the Flies"

BASA (FLAP)
BASA
......KUH! THE BLAST WAS BIGGER THAN I EXPECTED.
GOOOO (WOOOO)
......WE HAD A RENDEZ-VOUS POINT...BUT NOBODY CAME.
......
SHIJIMA, GUARD THE AREA.
I'M GONNA GO LOOK FOR THEM.
THEY MUST'VE GOTTEN OUT ALIVE.
KIIN (TIIING)

23rd Demon:
"Lord of the Flies"

*BELIEVE IN YOURSELF, HARUOMI—*

ゴォオオ
GOOOOO (WOOOO)
ブゥン
BUUN (VOOM)
ズル…
ZURU (SLIP)
UGH ......
SHUN (SWISH)
KUH ......
......

ZILCH, MY DAD ......
!

UM, UH...

......

IT TOOK EVERYTHING I HAD JUST TO GET THE TWO OF YOU OUT OF THERE.
I'M SORRY.

OH... I SEE.

THIS IS AWFUL... I MADE THE SAME MISTAKE TWICE.

AND THIS TIME... I LET THE PROFESSOR DIE...
IO... KUN.
...!
I'M SORRY... THIS TIME, I...
...WOULD NOT BLAME YOU FOR HATING ME AFTER WHAT I'VE DONE.
IF ONLY WE'D ESCAPED WITH TOUNOGI-SAN WHEN THE ALARMS FIRST STARTED GOING OFF...!

MURO-HIME...
WHEN IT COMES TO REPEAT BLUNDERS, I'M IN THE SAME BOAT AS YOU.
NOT ONLY COULD I NOT SAVE KAZUMA IO, I COULDN'T EVEN DEFEAT LERAJE.
GU (GRIP)
I'M TIRED OF HEARING PEOPLE CALL ME THE "PRINCE OF FEAR."
STOP IT, YOU TWO... I'M THE ONE WHO CAN'T DO ANYTHING.
BESIDES, MY DAD CAN'T BE DEAD—
YOUR FATHER IS DEAD.

BASASA (FLAP)
INDEED. HE HAS BEEN, WITHOUT A DOUBT, COMPLETELY AND UTTERLY...
...DISSOLVED AND MADE EXTINCT AT THE ATOMIC LEVEL.

Y-YOU...
HEL-LENTZA! WHY DID YOU...!?

LONG TIME NO SEE, ASTA-ROTH.
YOU STAY OUT OF THIS.
I'M TALKING TO HIM.

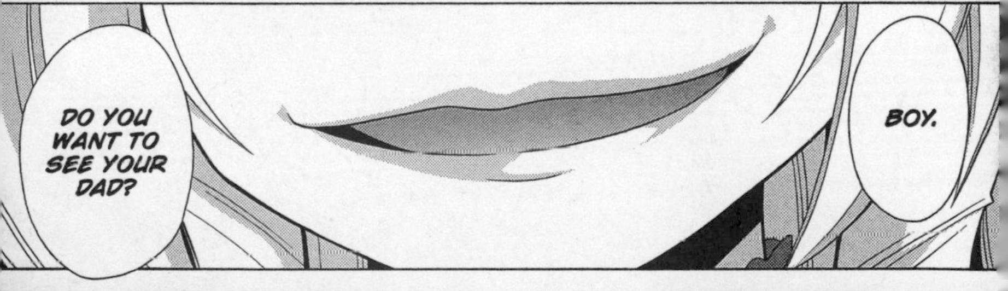
BOY.
DO YOU WANT TO SEE YOUR DAD?

WH... AT?

JUST LIKE I SAID. I'M NOT AS GOOD AS GAMIGIN OR BIFRONS, BUT I TOO CAN MANIPULATE THE SOULS OF THE DEAD.
YOU WISH TO SEE HIM?

.........
... DON'T, IO-KUN.

THIS IS HOW A DEMON LURES YOU IN— WITH SWEET WORDS ......
DON'T LEAVE YOUR FATHER'S SOUL IN THE HANDS OF A DEMON.

PROFESSOR IO WAS AN UPSTANDING MAN TO THE VERY END.
WE MUSTN'T DESECRATE YOUR FATHER'S SOUL!

YOU SAY HE WAS UPSTANDING TO THE END?
JUST THE SORT OF THING SOMEONE FROM THE CHURCH WOULD SAY, ELEVATING HIS ACTIONS TO A "NOBLE SACRIFICE."
UGH ......
GIRIRI (CHOKE)
DEATH IS NOTHING MORE THAN A NATURAL PHENOMENON.
MURO-HIME!?
LET GO OF MURO-HIME! SHE'S...
BA (BAH)
WHAT? YOU LIKE HER OR SOMETHING?
IT'S GOOD TO BE YOUNG AND NAIVE.
GU (TUG)

BIRII (RRRRIP)
TAKE A GOOD LOOK, THEN.
EE...

EEEEEEK !!
..........

SOPHIA-DONO, WHY IS HELLENTZA-SAMA SO INVESTED IN THAT BOY?
IS THAT HOW IT LOOKS TO YOU? WHY DO YOU THINK THAT IS?

NO IDEA.

YOU SAW HIM DEFLECT MY FLAMES, RIGHT?
HE'S CAPABLE OF INHUMAN FEATS.

THAT PERSON, HARUOMI IO-SAN, IS THE RING OF SOLOMON.
!

SOLOMON... THAT HAS A NOSTALGIC RING TO IT.
YES, IT DOES.

IN OTHER WORDS, WE SEVENTY-TWO "BRANCHES" DEFEAT HARUOMI-SAN.
BUT ......
... THAT'S A TREMENDOUS BURDEN.
IT EATS AWAY AT HIM, MENTALLY AND PHYSICALLY.
CAN HE REALLY CONQUER US?
GUNI (GROPE)
WELL, WELL. SUCH OBSCENE BREASTS YOU HAVE.
DON'T ...
THEY'RE EVEN BIGGER THAN MINE.
GUNI
MUNI (MOOSH)
AH ...!

...RIGHT NOW, I'M ABOUT READY TO SAY NOTHING AND GO HOME.
HANDS OFF MURO-HIME.

OH, COME NOW. YOU COULD TAKE MY PLACE.
PERO (LICK)
AND I COULD LET YOU MEET YOUR FATHER. DON'T BE SO RUDE.

BIKU (TWITCH)
NO...DON'T, IO-KUN...
YOU MUSTN'T LISTEN TO DEMONS ......

MURO-HIME ...!
I KNOW THIS IS COMING FROM ME AND ALL, BUT...
... YAKAGI'S RIGHT THIS TIME.

IF IT WAS JUST ABOUT COMMUNICATING WITH THE DEAD, THAT'D BE ONE THING. BUT A DEMON CAN MANIPULATE THE DEAD TO MAKE THEM SAY WHATEVER YOU WANT TO HEAR.
AS YOU CAN SEE, THIS HELLENTZA IS ONE WICKED BASTARD.

WHAT GIVES, ZILCH? IT HURTS ME THAT YOU'D CALL YOUR FORMER BEST FRIEND WICKED.
GOU (FWOOSH)
!
BA (BLOCK)
STUP—!
GUI (PUSH)
BO (FWOOSH)
...OH.
HEH HEH.
IO-KUN!
DON'T BE RECK-LESS! YOU'LL DIE!
WHAT THE...? THE POWER OF THE RING...
PUSU (SMOKE)
PUSU

YOU CAN'T STOP HER ATTACKS WITH THE RING.
SHE'S A NOBLE-MAN OF THE DEMON WORLD.
THE "LORD OF THE FLIES"—THE "BRANCH" OF BEELZEBUB.

NYA (SMIRK)
THE ONLY ONES YOU CAN CONQUER ARE THE SEVENTY-TWO "BRANCHES" KING SOLOMON SEALED AWAY.
BEELZE-BUB'S A WHOLE OTHER MATTER.
NOW THAT SHE MENTIONS IT, PRO-FESSOR LEVI DID SAY...
...THEY MADE A DEMON THAT THE RING CAN'T CONTROL INTO A "BRANCH" TOO...
I'LL KEEP HER BUSY.
YOU GET YAKAGI, HARU-OMI.
YOU STAND A CHANCE AT BEATING HER!?
WELL... WE'RE ABOUT EVEN.
BAN (BAM)

ZA (ZSH)
ZA
THAT'S IT. IT'S BEEN SO LONG SINCE WE'VE SEEN EACH OTHER...
...YOU STILL HAVEN'T GIVEN ME A HELLO HUG, ASTAROTH.
THEN I'LL HAVE TO PICK YOU UP AND SLAM YOU DOWN...
...LORD OF THE FLIES, BEELZEBUB!
ぽいっ
POI (TOSS)
VERY FUNNY.
EEK...!

BASHI (BSSHT)
NGH ...!
WHOA... THERE!
DO (WHUMP)
DOKI (THADUMP)

TH-THANK YOU... B-BUT PLEASE DON'T LOOK...
I-I'LL LEND YOU A SHIRT. JUST GIMME A SEC.
AH!
HEY, CHURCH GIRL! DROP THE BLUSHING DAMSEL ACT!
ブオン
BUON (BOOM)
QUIT PLAYING AROUND.
グイ
GUI (YANK)
OOH?

NUCHA (SHTICK)
ぬちゃ...

BAKU (GAPE)
EEEEEEEK!
UWAAAAAH!?

......

HELLENTZA-SAMA.
IS THIS OKAY WITH YOU?

...OH WELL.
I'LL HAVE ANOTHER OPPORTUNITY.

...I SEE. SO PROFESSOR IO IS GONE.

IT'S A SHAME.
YES...... AND IT'S DUE TO MY POOR JUDG-MENT.

WELL ...
...FIRST WE NEED TO GET HIM BACK ON HIS FEET.

NO, WE'RE ALL TO BLAME.
BUT WHAT MATTERS MOST IS WHAT WE DO NOW.
AND WHAT IS THAT?

SERIAL NUMBER 0047861, CODE SIGN "FOX 4"—YAKAGI MUROHIME.
FOR DISOBEYING YOUR ORDERS, THERE WILL BE A MORATORIUM ON ALL SPECIAL ACTIVITY PRIVILEGES.
24th Demon: Those Left Behind
AND YOU WILL BE TAKEN INTO CUSTODY.
...YES, SIR.
WAIT! IF SHE DISOBEYED ORDERS, THEN WE'RE JUST AS GUILTY...!
YAKAGI-KUN POSSESSES EXTRAORDINARY POWERS. EVEN IF YOU DISOBEYED THE SAME ORDERS, IT'S NOT THE SAME THING.
BUT!
FATHER PETERSEN.
I WAS PREPARED FOR THIS.

IT'S TRUE. I'M IN THE SAME POSITION AS IO-KUN.

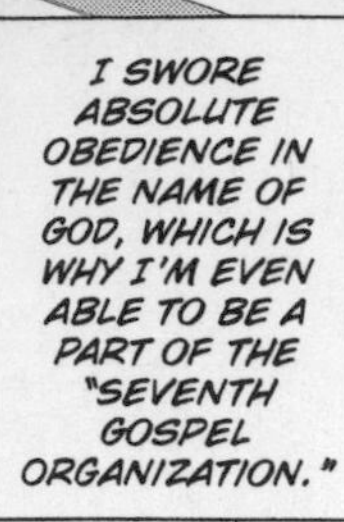
I SWORE ABSOLUTE OBEDIENCE IN THE NAME OF GOD, WHICH IS WHY I'M EVEN ABLE TO BE A PART OF THE "SEVENTH GOSPEL ORGANIZATION."

GASHAN (CLANK)
MY SUPER-POWERS ARE LIKE THOSE OF THE "BRANCHES" ...
THERE'S NO TELLING WHAT EFFECTS THEY COULD HAVE ON MY SURROUNDINGS WHEN I DISOBEY ORDERS AND USE THEM FOR PERSONAL REASONS.
BWEEEEP

THE CHURCH MUST BE FURIOUS WITH ME.
I BETRAYED THEM, LIKE JUDAS ISCARIOT.

...I HOPE IO-KUN'S OKAY...

24th Demon:
Those Left Behind

HOW COULD I HAVE BEEN SO RECK-LESS?
THE RING OF SOLOMON NEUTRAL-IZES AND CONQUERS THE POWER OF THE "BRANCHES."
DID I LOSE MYSELF IN THAT POWER?
ISN'T THAT HOW I LET MY FATHER DIE...?
SHIT ...!
......

HITA (PAD)
!

......YOU WERE RIGHT.
PEOPLE WHO GET INVOLVED WITH GOETIA DON'T GET OUT ALIVE.

THOUGH I WAS LEFT THERE MYSELF TEN YEARS AGO...
...AND EVEN LOST MY SISTER THERE.

BUT SINCE THIS *POWER* INSIDE ME...
...SOME-WHERE ALONG THE WAY, I GOT IT IN MY HEAD THAT I'D BE DIFFERENT.

WHAT IS WRONG WITH ME...? WAS I TRYING TO BE SOME KIND OF HERO?

SU (SWF)
...... HARU-OMI.
!

I DON'T CARE WHETHER YOU'RE A HERO OR NOT.
......
BUT IF YOU'RE GOING TO BE THE TRAGIC HERO, IT'LL END UP A COMEDY, SO JUST STOP.
IF YOU'VE GOT THE TIME TO LET KAZUMA IO'S DEATH MAKE YOU FEEL POWER-LESS...
...THEN DO YOUR JOB AS ONE OF THE LIVING.

YOU CARRY THE POWER AND MEMORIES THAT HE ENTRUSTED YOU.
AM I WRONG? HARUOMI IO.

KIIIN (TIIIING)
!
......STOP IT. I'M FINE.
TCH... IT POISONS THE BODY TO KEEP HOLDING IT IN AND POISONS THE HEART TO KEEP RESIST-ING.
IF I TOOK YOU UP ON YOUR OFFER... THAT'S WHEN I'D REALLY GET POISONED.
BUT I'LL AT LEAST ACCEPT THE SENTIMENT.

...BUT ZILCH.
HM?

WHAT DID MY DAD ACHIEVE?

EVEN IF THAT'S THE NOBLEST THING HE COULD HAVE DONE...

...FOR THOSE OF US LEFT BEHIND, WE ONLY FEEL THE LOSS.
Nff ...!
チュプ
CHAPU (SMACK)
......IF YOU DON'T KNOW, THEN GET "GAMIGIN" TO PUT YOU IN TOUCH WITH KAZUMA IO AND ASK HIM YOURSELF.
....... NAH, ONLY RIPE AT IM, SO LET'S NOT.

MY DAD'S GONE...
...SO I'M GONNA NEED YOU TO LOOK OUT FOR ME...
... PART-NER.
—SURE THING. YOU CAN COUNT ON ME.

NO, HE REALLY CAN'T.

IF MY BIG BROTHER RELIES ON YOU, HE'LL JUST END UP LIKE OUR DAD...

YOU AGAIN ...

?
WHAT'S WRONG ?

......NO. IT'S NOTHING.

WELL, OKAY THEN ......
CHANGA CHANGA CHAAANGA CHANG ♪

HI, THIS IS IO.
This is Tounogi. If you're at your house, then get out right away.

The Seventh Gospel Organization will be raiding it soon.

THE CHURCH? THAT'S ...
HARU-OMI.

-CLICK-CLICK-CLANK-CLANK-

BAN (BAM)

FOX 10 TO HQ. BOTH TARGETS HAVE ESCAPED.
RE-QUESTING MALOUX TO PURSUE THEM.

HQ to Fox 10.
Maloux is currently on vacation.

...I KNEW IT.
SO THAT PRIEST WAS HOLDING OUT ON US.
BOOOO (DAZE)
ぼー…
ZILCH?
HUH? OH. RIGHT.
THE CHURCH IS CRAFTY.
YOU OKAY? YOU DON'T LOOK SO GOOD...
YOU TWO ALL RIGHT!?

...... LOOKS LIKE YOU'RE FINE.
ZA (ZSH)
HATO, YOU TOO...?
YEAH. I WAS HOME WHEN THE CHURCH RAIDED IT.
MY ADDRESS WAS PROBABLY LEAKED BY MUROHIME-SAN.
EITHER WAY, I'M JUST GLAD YOU'RE OKAY, HATO.
MM, OKAY ...... SURE.

COME ON! WE'RE GOING TO TOUNOGI'S PLACE THIS INSTANT, BLOCK-HEAD!
BOKA (BONK)
OW! WHAT WAS THAT FOR!?

...SIGH. WE FAILED.

WHAT'S THE MATTER, TOU-NOGI-SAN?
OH. HARUOMI-KUN, THAT YOU?

PRO-FESSOR LEVI WON'T COME OUT.
I CAN *SEE* HER COLOR, SO SHE'S DEFINITELY THERE, BUT...
...SHE WON'T RE-SPOND.

SIGN: FIRE EXTINGUISHER

... RIGHT.
MY HEAD UNDER-STANDS IT.

BUT I WONDER IF I'LL BE ABLE TO COME UP WITH THE RIGHT WORDS, THE WAY I FEEL NOW.
BUN (VOOM)
ZO (ZOOSH)
ZO

ZA (ZSH)
ZA
ZA

PRO-FES-SOR LEVI.
ARE YOU IN?

...YOU ARE, AREN'T YOU.
GOSO (RUMMAGE)

...PRO-
FESSOR...
LEVI.

...OH,
HARUOMI-
KUN.

...I'M SORRY...I COULDN'T ...SAVE HIM...
WHY ARE YOU APOLOGIZING...?

FIRST YOUR MOTHER, THEN YOUR SISTER, AND NOW YOUR FATHER ......
YOU SHOULD BE A LOT MORE TORN UP THAN ME, DON'T YOU THINK?

YOU'RE RIGHT...
... BUT...

...HE LEFT ME SOMETHING TO KEEP ME FROM GETTING OVERWHELMED BY IT.

I NEED YOUR HELP TOO, PROFESSOR LEVI.

YOU'RE SO STRONG, HARUOMI-KUN...
......BUT.

DOSA (WHUMP)
BUT I'M... NOT THAT STRONG.

PRO-FESSOR LEVI......?

25th Demon: Corrosion

WHAT'RE YOU TALKING ABOUT? YOU'RE THE ONE WHO SAID IO-KUN SHOULD GO.
GU (GRAB)
AND WHO'RE YOU CALLING YOUR BROTHER?
PASHI (SMACK)
!
DON'T TOUCH ME.
HOW DARE A NOBODY LIKE YOU MAKE EYES AT MY BROTHER, GAMIGIN.
ASTAROTH...... NO.

WHO... ARE YOU?

UM...
...PRO-
FESSOR
LEVI...
GOKU (GULP)
ゴクッ...

LOOKS LIKE YOU'RE IN TROUBLE, HARUOMI IO...
SITRI.
IF I WERE THE ONE HANDLING A WOMAN'S SEX DRIVE, I'D TAKE CARE OF IT LICKETY-SPLIT.
SHUT UP AND GET OUT OF HERE!
DON'T WASTE THIS OPPORTUNITY TO GET WITH AN OLDER WOMAN.
IF YOU KEEP THAT UP, YOU'LL NEVER LOSE YOUR VIRGINITY, RING OF SOLOMON.
HEE HEE.
SHUUU (SSSHHH)
.........
PROFESSOR... LEVI.
...I'M SORRY. EVEN THOUGH YOU HAVE IT SO TOUGH, HARUOMI-KUN...
...AND I SHOULD GET IT TOGETHER...

...WE'VE BOTH LOST SOMEONE DEAR TO US.

SO LET'S STOP PUSHING IT. IT'D MAKE MY DAD SAD TOO.

...... THANK YOU.

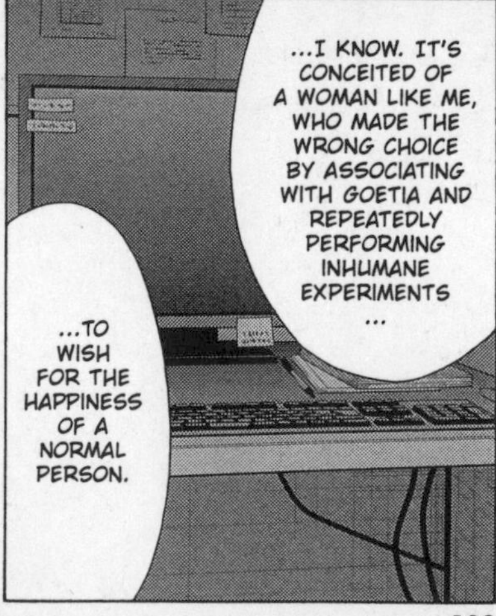
...I KNOW. IT'S CONCEITED OF A WOMAN LIKE ME, WHO MADE THE WRONG CHOICE BY ASSOCIATING WITH GOETIA AND REPEATEDLY PERFORMING INHUMANE EXPERIMENTS ...
...TO WISH FOR THE HAPPINESS OF A NORMAL PERSON.

SOMEDAY, I'LL ALSO GET WHAT'S COMING TO ME...
BUT THAT'S NOT WHAT SCARES ME.

I'M SCARED OF NOT ACCOMPLISHING ANYTHING AND IT ALL BEING POINTLESS...
スッ SU (SWF)

THERE ARE THINGS ONLY YOU CAN DO, PROFESSOR LEVI.
AND IF YOU KEEP REPENTING FOR ALL YOUR MISTAKES AND MAKE UP FOR THEM...
...I'M SURE YOU'LL BE FORGIVEN.

BY MY DAD, YOURSELF...
...AND EVEN "ASTAROTH," ZILCH, SOMEDAY.

THANK YOU...
THAT WAS JUST WHAT I NEEDED TO HEAR...

WHO EXACTLY IS GOING TO FORGIVE YOU?
ZIL... CH?

THEY DID TERRIBLE THINGS TO US AND LET COUNTLESS OTHERS DIE......
BUT THEN WHEN SOMEONE CLOSE TO HER DIES, SHE'S HEART-BROKEN?
WHOA, ZILCH...
......
WHO WOULD EVER FORGIVE SOMEONE LIKE THAT?
GIVE ME A BREAK!!

... YOU'RE RIGHT. I HAVE NO PLACE TO RUN.
ALL I CAN DO IS WAIT FOR THE DAY MY SENTENCE IS PASSED WHILE I APOLOGIZE TO ALL THOSE CHILDREN I SACRIFICED.
IN THAT CASE ...
SHA (SWISH)
!!
DIE, RIGHT HERE AND NOW.
GU (GRAB)
THE WATCHER EGGS ARE WAITING FOR YOU.

STOP, ZILCH!
WHAT'S GOTTEN INTO YOU TODAY!?
NOTHING!!
DON'T YOU THINK YOU'RE THE ONE ACTING WEIRD, ONII-CHAN!?
WE WERE KILLED TEN YEARS AGO, OKAY!?
AND PEOPLE KEEP DYING EVEN NOW!
HOW CAN YOU BE OKAY WITH THIS!?

ZILCH, YOU'RE
......

WHO.........ARE YOU?

... UGH...
AGH...
GIRI (CHOKE)

AH!

THAT'S ENOUGH, STOP IT! ARE YOU CRAZY!?
GA (GRAB)

I DON'T WANT TO USE THE POWER OF THE RING ON YOU.
GU (TUG)
ZILCH!
I...

THAT IS...
...NOT MY NAME!!
BA (WHIP)
BUN (SWING)
GOO (WHOOSH)

GA (GRAB)
GIN (TING)
...I KNEW IT. YOU WERE INSIDE ME...
...WEREN'T YOU?

TOBARI.
......OH. I GUESS I DIDN'T DIE.
I LOST OUT, SAVING YOU.
WELL, YOU OWE ME ONE.
BACHI (ZAP)
GYU (SQUEEZE)
HYAH ...!

ZILCH!!
ZUSHA (CRASH)
ズルル… ZURURU (SLIDE)
PRO-FES-SOR LEVI!
...DO WHAT YOU WILL NOW, HARUOMI IO.
OKAY! THANKS, TOBARI!
ZA (CZSH)
ZA
ZA
WORDS OF THANKS...
I HAVEN'T HEARD THOSE FOR A LONG TIME.
PRO-FES-SOR LEVI!
SHU (SHWIP)
I'M FINE... GO CHECK ON ZILCH-CHAN.

OH... UH.
ZILCH, YOU OKAY ...?
...WHAA—?
WHAT HAP-PENED? WHAT WAS I DOING? ...... WHERE AM I?
.........
COULD IT BE...? NAH.
THERE'S NO WAY ......

......
MASTER,
WE...
YEAH
...

KUH
......

ZILCH-KUN SUDDENLY PULLED A FAST ONE ON US...
よろ
YORO
(TEETER)
SHIT... CURSE THAT ASTAROTH ...!

ZILCH-KUN WAS CLEARLY NOT NORMAL... WHAT WAS THAT...?
BUUUU
(BZZZ)
ブーーッ
ブーーッ
BUUUU

FATHER PETERSEN?

WHAT'S GOING TO HAPPEN TO ME NOW?
IO-KUN...
...I WANT TO SEE YOU AGAIN...

RUN AWAY FROM HERE.
!!
BA (JUMP)
YOU'RE GOING TO BE KILLED...
...BY ASTAROTH'S "BRANCH."

WHO...
...ARE YOU?

26th Demon
Eclipse Level

THE "LAND OF TWILIGHT" ...
...STANDS IN THE SPACE BETWEEN THE REAL WORLD AND THE DEMON WORLD.
VERY IMPRESSIVE, "DECEPTIVE GENERALISSIMO MALPHAS."
I COMPLETED THE OUTSIDE IN JUST A DAY.
THE INTERIOR EXPERIMENT EQUIPMENT WAS SO SPECIALIZED THAT IT TOOK A LOT OF TIME AND MONEY.
JUST WHAT ONE WOULD EXPECT FROM THE DEMON WORLD'S FOREMOST ARCHITECT.
WITH THIS, IT'LL BE HARD FOR EVEN OUR ENEMIES TO DETECT US.
WE'VE ALREADY LOST OUR INFORMATION FEE FROM THE CHURCH, THOOOUGH.

HOWEVER, ALMOST ALL THE BRANCHES AND 90% OF GOETIA'S FAR EAST PERSONNEL HAVE GONE OVER TO HELLENTZA-SAMA'S SIDE.
I DON'T THINK THERE'LL BE ANY OBSTACLES TO OUR ACTIVITIES.

—SO WHAT DO WE DO NOW?

BEELZE-BUB-SAMA?
I'M GLAD YOU ASKED.

LIVING AS A "BRANCH" SHOULD BE AMUSING.
I THINK I'LL RESEARCH IT A LITTLE MORE.
I'M CURIOUS TO SEE IF WE CAN ATTAIN "PROJECT EDEN" OR WHATEVER IT'S CALLED.
YOU MEAN THAT PLAN ABOUT MAKING THAT HEAVENLY PRESENCE A "BRANCH" TOO...?
HUMANS THINK UP THE CRAZIEST THINGS.

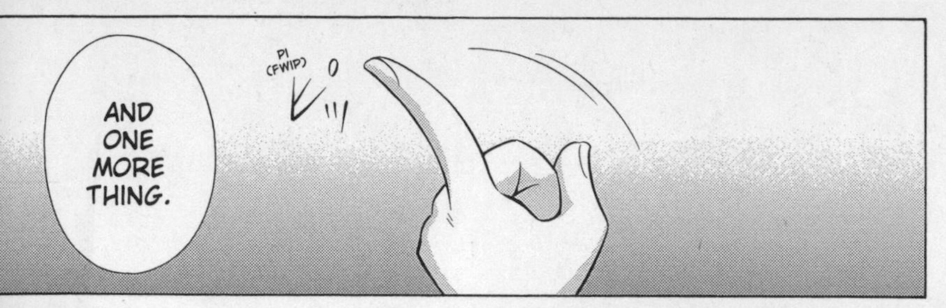
PI (FWIP)
AND ONE MORE THING.

THE MISSING DEMON LORD, "LUCIFER."

HE IS TRUE ORDER.
IF WE'RE GOING TO CONQUER AND REMAIN HERE, WE NEED HIM.

GOETIA TRIED TO TURN EVEN LUCIFER INTO A "BRANCH"... AND FAILED. THAT'S AS FAR AS THE RECORDS SHOW.
I HAVE NO IDEA WHAT OCCURRED AFTER THAT.
AND WE ALREADY KNOW HE'S NOT IN JUDECCA.

OH WELL. KNOWING LUCIFER, HE'D LAUGH AT ME FOR WORRYING SO MUCH.
BESIDES, WE HAVE SOMETHING BIGGER TO WORRY ABOUT.

THE ONE CAPABLE OF SUBJUGATING US SEVENTY-TWO DEMONS......
THAT BOY.

.........

HARUOMI IO...YOU MEAN.

*I SEE. THAT WOMAN...... I MIGHT BE ABLE TO USE HER.*

—ONII-CHAN...

ONII-CHAN...

WHO'S THERE? "BROTHER"? YOU MEAN ME?

HOW COULD YOU FORGET, ONII-CHAN?

YOU PROMISED.

PROMISED...

YOU PROMISED WE'D ALWAYS BE TOGETHER. THAT YOU'D PROTECT ME.

THAT'S RIGHT, I DID...I PROMISED MY LITTLE SISTER... AYANA...

BUT YOU'RE NOT HER.

YOU'RE ZILCH.

ZAZA (FZZT)

—MI-KUN. HARUOMI-KUN.

NGH ......
ARE YOU AWAKE?

HATO ...?
MORNING... I'VE BEEN UP ALL NIGHT.

SORRY. WE WERE THE ONLY ONES TO FALL ASLEEP ......
DID YOU FIND ANYTHING FROM THE DATA TOUNOGI-SAN OBTAINED ...?
ZZZ...
ZZZ...
YES ...

IT WAS PASSWORD PROTECTED AND ENCRYPTED, SO I'VE ONLY BEEN ABLE TO READ A SMALL PART OF IT...
I KNOW YOU JUST WOKE UP, HARUOMI-KUN, BUT...

...DO YOU REMEMBER...
...ANOTHER LITTLE GIRL WHO WAS ALWAYS WITH YOU BESIDES YOUR LITTLE SISTER IN GOETIA...?

JITO (STARE)
UH... YEAH.
SHE WAS ANOTHER WATCHER EGG.

......YEAH. SHE WAS DEFINITELY THERE. THE THREE OF US WERE ALWAYS TOGETHER.
......HUH?

...WHO WAS SHE? I CAN'T REMEMBER HER NAME.

IT'S LIKE... THERE'S SOMETHING I DON'T WANT TO REMEMBER...
...SOMETHING THAT WOULD BE BAD IF I DID...

...I'M SORRY. I CAN'T REMEMBER HER NAME.
I SEE...YOU PROBABLY DON'T KNOW THIS, BUT...

...SHE AND YOUR LITTLE SISTER, AYANA-CHAN, WERE REMARKABLY COMPATIBLE WITH THE "BRANCHES" OUT OF ALL THE WATCHER EGGS. THEY WERE LABELED AS "ECLIPSE LEVEL" CHILDREN.
AYANA-CHAN IN PARTICULAR HAD A LOT OF EXPECTATIONS PLACED ON HER SINCE SHE WAS THE CHILD OF THE PROFESSORS IO.
BUT RESEARCHERS OUTSIDE OF PROFESSOR IO'S TEAM APPARENTLY COULDN'T EVEN MAKE A PASS AT AYANA-KUN.
SO FIRST THEY STARTED WITH YOUR CHILDHOOD FRIEND...
...OR MORE LIKE THEY *ATTEMPTED* TO START WITH HER.
*HER NAME WAS AKINO KIRIBA.*
RING A BELL?
*AKINO...*

OH, THAT'S RIGHT. THAT WAS HER NAME.

WE WERE CLOSE.

I LIKED HER... I THINK?

—SO WHY COULDN'T I REMEMBER UNTIL NOW?

NO. SHE DID DIE...
IN THAT EXPLOSION DURING THE MIDDLE OF THE EXPERIMENT, ALONG WITH MY MOM AND LITTLE SISTER.
!? ...... AM I WRONG ABOUT THAT TOO?
...WHAT? I FEEL LIKE I SHOULDN'T HEAR ANY MORE...
YOU OKAY? THERE'S STILL MORE.
I SHOULDN'T BE HEARING THIS. THOUGH I CAN'T DENY SOMETHING'S GOT ME HOOKED...
A NUMBER OF RESEARCH TEAMS AT THE TIME GOT CARRIED AWAY. I WAS IN A DIFFERENT TEAM SO I HAD NO IDEA, BUT...
...SOMEHOW, IT APPEARS AKINO-CHAN MANAGED TO NARROWLY ESCAPE DEATH.
BUT OF COURSE IT LEFT HER IN NO SHAPE TO ENDURE FURTHER EXPERIMENTS.

SO IN HER PLACE... AYANA-CHAN WAS USED.
......
AYA... NA...
THEN AYANA WAS—
AKINO WAS—

WE STILL HAVEN'T FOUND ANY DATA ON AYANA-CHAN.
IT'S EITHER IN AN ENCRYPTED FILE OR PROFESSOR IO ERASED IT.
GI (CREAK)
THIS IS PROBABLY VERY CONFUSING FOR YOU, BUT THERE'S EVEN MORE WE'VE LEARNED.
!

AKINO KIRIBA ESCAPED DEATH BY A HAIR'S BREADTH, BUT...SHE WAS A VALUABLE ECLIPSE LEVEL.
SHE UNDERWENT A LENGTHY RECOVERY AND AFTER A NUMBER OF YEARS WAS MADE A TEST SAMPLE ONCE AGAIN.

IT WAS A TEST TO FUSE HER WITH LUCIFER OF ALL THINGS.
!
THAT'S THE HEIGHT OF RECK-LESS-NESS.

......HUH? THIS GIRL...
ZUI (PRESS)
......

AKINO KIR
THE EXPERIMENT HAPPENED THREE YEARS AGO AND, SURE ENOUGH, WAS A FAILURE...
THE RESULTING WIDE-SCALE EXPLOSION CAUSED GOETIA TO LOSE MORE PERSONNEL AND MATERIAL THAN EVEN THE ACCIDENT TEN YEARS PRIOR.
HER POTENTIAL WAS DEEMED SUFFICIENT, BUT UNFORTUNATELY, HE WAS TOO MUCH FOR HER.
I CAN'T REMEMBER ANYTHING FROM BEFORE THREE YEARS AGO. NOT WHO I WAS OR WHERE I CAME FROM.
THEN THE ACCIDENT THREE YEARS AGO... I CAUSED AS A TEST SUBJECT.

THAT GIRL...
AKINO WAS—
YAKAGI MURO-HIME!

—I DON'T ASK FOR MUCH, BUT... YOU SHOULD KEEP A CLOSE EYE ON ZILCH-KUN.

...I WILL.

... YOU'VE SURE GOT IT TOUGH TOO.

YOU KNOW ALREADY, DON'T YOU?
...... KNOW WHAT?

WHAT HAPPENED A FEW MONTHS AFTER THE ACCIDENT THREE YEARS AGO.
A FEMALE AGENT WITH SUPER-NATURAL POWERS SUDDENLY SHOWED UP AND STARTED WORKING FOR THE SEVENTH GOSPEL ORGANIZATION.

YOU DON'T HAVE TO ASK ME HER NAME. YOU ALREADY KNOW.
BUT THAT'S JUST A MADE-UP NAME THE CHURCH GAVE HER.

I DON'T KNOW WHAT WENT DOWN BETWEEN YOU TWO IN THE PAST.
......
NEITHER OF YOU REALIZED YOU WERE MEETING EACH OTHER AGAIN. SURE IS COMPLI-CATED.

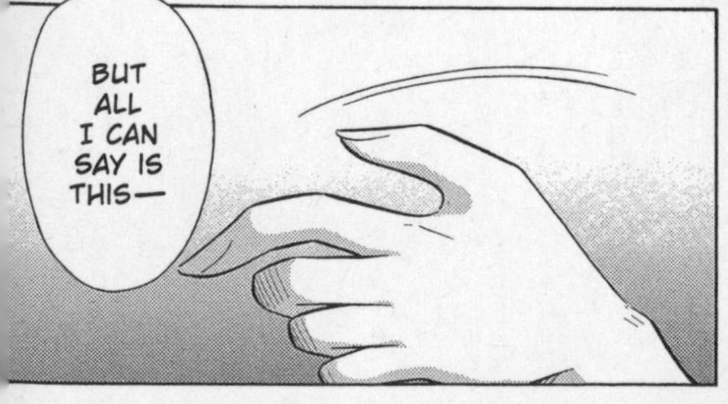
BUT ALL I CAN SAY IS THIS—

YOU WANT TO SAVE HER.
YOU WANT TO GET HER BACK.
RIGHT?
!!
I HEARD FROM FATHER PETER-SEN.
RIGHT NOW, YAKAGI-KUN'S BEING KEPT A PRISONER IN THE CHURCH.
SEEMS SHE'LL BE SENT TO THE HEAD-QUARTERS AT THE VATICAN BEFORE LONG.
MURO-HIME...?
SURE, SHE DISOBEYED HER ORDERS, BUT...
...THAT STILL DOESN'T WARRANT...

......I KNOW HOW YOU FEEL.
I HAVE SOMEONE I WANT TO SAVE TOO.
YOU'RE GOING, RIGHT?
OF COURSE.
THIS TIME FOR SURE.
I'M GONNA SAVE HER!

27th Demon:
Murohime Recovered
MOGU (CHEW) もぐ
MOGU もぐ
...ARE YOU GOING TO EAT TOO?
...I GUESS NOT.

...REMEMBER ...HURRY.

DON'T RUSH ME.
I KNOW I HAVEN'T MADE MUCH OF AN EFFORT TO RE-MEMBER ANY-THING, THOUGH.

EVER SINCE A FEW DAYS AGO, VISIONS OF THIS LITTLE GIRL HAVE SUDDENLY STARTED POPPING UP.
I TRIED ASKING THE SECURITY PERSONNEL AND MALOUX, BUT IT SEEMS I REALLY AM THE ONLY ONE WHO CAN SEE HER.

MY EXPERIENCE IN GOETIA MUST HAVE TRIGGERED SOMETHING IN ME.
I'M SANE. I MAY BE SHACKLED AND KEPT IN SOLITARY CONFINE-MENT, BUT...
...I'M STILL FREE TO BATHE AND USE THE TOILET, AND I'M GIVEN A FORK AND KNIFE FOR MY MEALS TOO.

LUCKILY, I STILL HAVE FATHER PETER-SEN AND MALOUX AND MANY OTHER ALLIES ON MY SIDE.
I'M NOT BEING TOLD I'VE LOST MY MIND. I'M OKAY.

27th Demon:
Murohime Recovered

......
OKAY.
HOW DO
WE GET
IN FROM
HERE?
MAYBE
WE REALLY
SHOULD HAVE
WAITED FOR
SHIJIMA AND
THE OTHER
TO FULLY
RECOVER,
YOU KNOW?
......
IT'LL
BE TOO
LATE IF WE
WAIT UNTIL
AFTER
MUROHIME'S
BEEN
SHIPPED
OUT...
I HAVE
TO TALK
TO HER.
GASA
(RUSTLE)
THERE'S
NO
NEED TO
RUSH IT,
THOUGH.
ZA
(ZSH)
GOOD
GRIEF.

SHALL WE LEND YOU A HAND, HARUOMI IO?
I'VE NEVER BEEN INSIDE A CHURCH, SO I'M ACTUALLY LOOKING FORWARD TO IT......
ARE THESE... THE "BRANCHES" UNDER YOUR CONTROL?
THEY'RE NOT "BRANCHES," BUT APPARENTLY HONEST-TO-GOODNESS DEMONS NOW...
I TECHNICALLY CONQUERED THEM, BUT WITH HOW THEY'LL SHOW UP WHENEVER THEY WANT, IT MAKES ME WONDER IF THEY REALLY EVEN ARE UNDER MY CONTROL.
O-OH, I SEE...
WELL, IF YOU'RE GOING TO TELL US TO STAY PUT, THEN HOW ABOUT... YOU SHOW US YOUR SKILLS...?

EITHER WAY, YOU'VE BEEN CHASED OUT OF THE CHURCH.
WHY DON'T WE USE THESE GIRLS TO MAKE A REAL SHOW OF IT?
PERSONALLY, I'D LIKE TO GO ABOUT THIS AS PEACEFULLY AS POSSIBLE...
BASA
BASA (FLAP)
NOW THERE'S MORE OF THEM...
THIS IS THE FUR-THEST THING FROM A COINCI-DENCE.
WELL, WELL! WHAT A COINCIDENCE, HARUOMI-SAN.
GOOD EVENIIIING.
BASA
WHAT DO YOU WANT, AMON !?
FWEH...! PLEASE. CALL ME SOPHIA.

...I CAN'T BELIEVE THE "MARQUIS OF FLAME" HAS BEEN REDUCED TO THIS WEAK LITTLE "BRANCH"...
TERE TERE (SHY) てれてれ
EH-HEH-HEH! THANK YOU MUCH.
THAT WASN'T A COMPLIMENT.
IN ANY CASE, WOULD THE TWO OF YOU GET BACK INSIDE ME...?

......SO. HARUOMI-SAN.

DO YOU HAVE SOME BUSINESS WITH THE CHURCH OR SOMETHING? WHY ARE YOU SNEAKING AROUND OUT HERE?
......IT'S COMPLICATED.

A LOT'S HAPPENED, AND NOW I'M NO LONGER WORKING WITH THE CHURCH.

REALLY?
REALLY.

YAY! THEN WHY DON'T YOU JOIN OUR SIDE?
WAH!!
BA (GLOMP)
ばっ
AS OF NOW, WE ALREADY HAVE SEVERAL DOZEN "BRANCHES" ON OUR SIDE.
AND OF COURSE, ME TOO... ♡
GUGIG! (STRAIN)
ぐぎぎ
WAIT, WAIT, WAIT, WAIT!
MY NECK!!
YOU'RE NOT SATISFIED WITH ME? BUT I'M THE BIGGEST OF THE BUNCH.
MUNI (PRESS)
むにぃ
MUNYUN
むにゅん
......(IN WHAT REGARD?)
I HEAR YOU WORK FOR BEELZE-BUB.
WHAT'S IN IT FOR HARUOMI-KUN IF HE JOINS YOU GUYS?
THE SEVENTY-TWO "BRANCHES" CAN BE HELPFUL.

FOR EXAAAMPLE...
... NOTHING OUT OF THE ORDINARY HERE.
BUT EVEN IF THE ORDERS ARE FROM THE VATICAN, I CAN'T BE-LIEVE WE'RE SENDING THEM OUR MOST CAPABLE, MUROHIME ...
OUR ORGANI-ZATION'S FULL OF TOO MANY SMALL FRIES.
WHAT ELSE DO YOU EXPECT?
GYUOO (WHOOSH)
IT'S FILLED WITH NOBODIES WHO CAN'T EVEN HANDLE DIRECTLY MAKING A MOVE ON GOETIA.
BY THE WAY, WHERE'S THAT YAKAGI MUROHIME AT?

DOO (BOOM)
!!

SHE'S HERE, SHE'S HERE, SHE'S HERE! COME ON! GO ON INSIDE!
IT SHOULD BE A MADHOUSE IN THERE RIGHT NOW!
BA (BAH)
OOOOO (WOOOOO)
DIDN'T I JUST SAY I WANTED TO GO ABOUT THIS PEACE-FULLY!?
AND YOU MEAN TO SAY THIS IS YOUR DOING!

WELL, THIS CER-TAINLY IS OUR CHANCE.
LEAVE THE PRIESTS TO ME. YOU GO TO YAKAGI-KUN!
ARE YOU GONNA BE OKAY TAKING ON THOSE PRIESTS?

I DIDN'T TELL YOU THIS, BUT THE DATA I STOLE...
...INCLUDED A TRUMP CARD THAT'S PRETTY INCONVENIENT FOR THEM.

GOOOOO (WOOOOO)
I'M GOING TO USE THAT, SO NO NEED TO WORRY.
OKAY. THEN SEE YOU LATER!

ZAAAAA (SSSHHH)
SHAAAAAAA (SSSSHHH)
...I KNOW YOU'RE WATCHING, MALOUX.
IF YOU RECORD THIS, YOU'RE DEAD MEAT.
......... THAT REMINDS ME.
HEH HEH.
UH HEH HEH HEH HEH HEH!
IO-KUN SAW ME NAKED...
THOUGH THERE WAS NOTHING I COULD DO ABOUT IT.

N-NOW I CAN NEVER BECOME A BRIDE...!
BO (BLUSH)
ぼっ
ズズゥン…
ZUZUUN (THOOOOM)
!
ドゴォ
DOGOO (BOOM)
EEK—!
PARA
パラ
PARA (FLAKE)
パラ
WH-WHA...
WHAT'S GOING ON...?
NOW... RUN ......
BOU (GLOW)
ぼう…
!!

YOU......
DO (BLAM)
DO
DO
DO
BOGOO (BOOM)
UWAH!
HYUN (ZIP)
HYUN
DOKA (STAB)
!!

MONSTERS... WE WON'T LET YOU DO AS YOU PLEASE IN THIS SACRED PLACE OF WORSHIP.
GOOOO (WOOO)
TAKE THE INJURED INSIDE!
AND JUST WHO DO YOU THINK ...
... BROUGHT THOSE MON-STERS INTO THE WORLD?
!

HAIME TOUNOGI ...
WELL, WELL. EVEN THOUGH TODAY ISN'T SUNDAY WORSHIP, THINGS CERTAINLY ARE LIVELY IN HERE.

GIRLS, WE ADULTS NEED TO TALK.
......
ZURU (SLIDE)
YOU MIND KEEPING IT DOWN?

...I KNEW IT. SO YOU WERE COLLUDING WITH DEMONS.
NO, NO. NOT COLLUD-ING. USING THEM. JUST USING THEM.

THESE GIRLS YOU CALL MONSTERS ...
...WERE CALLED *VICTIMS* NOT TOO LONG AGO.

POOR CHILDREN USED AND ABUSED BY GOETIA.
AND WHAT IS GOETIA?

GOETIA WAS NOTHING MORE THAN A LOCATION WHERE PEOPLE WITH BIZARRE TASTES AND DEVIL WORSHIPPERS GATHERED. SO HOW DO YOU SUPPOSE IT EVOLVED INTO SUCH A LARGE ORGANIZATION?
*BECAUSE THERE WAS SOMEONE BEHIND THE CURTAIN FUNDING AND STAFFING IT.*

... WHAT ARE YOU GETTING AT?
THE SEVENTH GOSPEL ORGANIZATION'S MISSION IS TO DISPOSE OF THE "BRANCHES" FACILITY, GOETIA.
THE INVESTIGATION TO FIND THE SUPPORTER BEHIND IT IS BEING CARRIED OUT BY THE "THIRD GOSPEL ORGANIZATION"!

HEH...
...I CAN'T BELIEVE A MIDDLE MANAGEMENT ORGANIZATION COULD BE SO PATHETIC.

THE SUPPORTER OF GOETIA IS THE THIRD GOSPEL ORGANIZA-TION.
NOT YOU, AN AFFILIATED GROUP, BUT ONE UNDER THE DIRECT SUPER-VISION OF THE VATICAN ITSELF.
THE HEAD OF THE GOETIA FAR EAST LABORATORY, HUBERT EMERAN...
OF COURSE, THAT'S JUST AN ALIAS. STORY IS HE USED TO BE A PRIEST WITH THE VATICAN.
TALK ABOUT DISPATCHING THEIR WORK-FORCE, EH?

BUT NOW EMERAN'S DEAD, AND FROM WHAT HARUOMI-KUN AND HIS FRIENDS SAY, THE "BRANCH" OF BEELZEBUB NOW HOLDS THE REAL POWER.
THE THIRD GOSPEL ORGANIZATION MUST BE IN A PANIC.

...YOU EXPECT US TO BELIEVE THAT STORY?
NOT AT ALL.

I'LL GIVE YOU THE DATA I COPIED ON-SITE.
THE RAW VERSION BEFORE I ANALYZED THE ENCRYPTION AND HAD ANY TIME TO FALSIFY.
SA (SWF)

ANYWAY, WHAT I'M TRYING TO SAY IS THIS.
WE'RE LEAVING?
MM-HM.

YOU CAN'T HAND OVER HARUOMI-KUN AND YAKAGI-KUN...
...TO THOSE DETESTABLE VILLAINS.

...GOING IN WITH GUNS BLAZING—
WERE YOU EXCITED TO FIGHT IT OUT WITH THE CHURCH STAFF?
NO. AND I'M ACTUALLY GOING A LOT EASIER ON THEM SINCE HELLENTZA-SAMA SPECIFICALLY ORDERED THAT WE KEEP CASUALTIES TO A MINIMUM.

HUH. HOW COME?
I GET THE IMPRESSION IT HAS TO DO WITH MUROHIME-SAN.
YOU KNOW.
...I SEE.
SO IT'S ACTUALLY MUROHIME YOU'RE AFTER!!
DA (DASH)
DA
AAAH! WAIT! PLEASE WAIT!!

HARU-KUN...!

HARU-KUN!
DA DA DA DA DA
ダダダダダッ
AKINO ...!?
AKINO, WHAT'RE YOU DOING HERE...?
WHY ARE YOU......?
BACK THEN, I—
HARUOMI-SAAAN...
...YOU OKAY ...?

......
AKINO?
...HUH?
...I MEAN—MURO-HIME... YOU......

ALL THIS TIME ...
GYU (HUG)
ALL THIS TIME, YOU'VE BEEN ALIVE ...!

HUH? WHAT? WAIT... I'M... NAKED.
WH-WHAT'S IO-KUN DOING HERE ......?

MAYBE...
...HE CAME TO SAVE ME...?

TO BE CONTINUED

A LOT HAPPENED IN 2016. LIKE THE TEN-YEAR ANNIVERSARY SINCE MY DEBUT (MISREPRESENTING MY PERSONAL HISTORY). BUT THE BIGGEST EVENTS WERE GETTING MARRIED AND STARTING A NEW HOME TOGETHER. IN THE ENDNOTES OF VOLUME 3, I WROTE ABOUT WHAT I'D LOST, BUT NOW I'M THINKING OF EVERYTHING THAT CAN BE GAINED IN ONE'S LIFE. YEP.
AND WITH THAT, THIS WILL CONTINUE ON IN VOLUME 5.
NOVEMBER 2016
MILAN MATRA
■ ASSISTANTS
YOSHIMASA ASAYAMA
YUNOMI KUMATSU
■ COVER ILLUSTRATION COLORING
"MALPHAS" DESIGN &
NAGU KAGURAZAKA
(NAMES LISTED WITHOUT HONORIFICS)

I'M GOING HOME.
TO THAT EMPTINESS.
TO THAT LIGHT-FILLED HEAVEN!
I DON'T KNOW.
MY MEMORIES ARE DENYING ME.
WHAT FATE IS FAST APPROACHING FOR THE CHILDREN WHO WERE SACRIFICED TO THE POWER OF DEMONS!?
DON'T THINK THAT THINGS WILL GO AS YOU EXPECT...
...ASTA-ROTH.
YOU'VE BEEN HAD.
IT WAS NEVER THERE FROM THE VERY START.

AS LONG AS LUCIFER'S ALL RIGHT, THAT'S ALL I NEED.
CIMERIES. HAAGENTI. MURMUR. GO!
THE STORY HEADS FOR A CLIMAX CENTERED AROUND MURO-HIME AND ZILCH!!
I'LL KILL HER.
WHY IS THAT GIRL...
I'LL KILL HER.
...GETTING IN MY WAY?
I'LL KILL HER.
I'LL KILL HER.
Demonizer Zilch Volume 5 Coming Soon!!
THIS IS JUST A PREVIEW. THERE'S NO GUARANTEE THAT THIS IS WHAT VOLUME 5 WILL ACTUALLY BE LIKE (HEH).

# DEMONIZER ZILCH 4

## MILAN MATRA

Translation: Christine Dashiell • Lettering: Phil Christie



Yen Press
1290 Avenue of the Americas
New York, NY 10104

Visit us at yenpress.com
facebook.com/yenpress
twitter.com/yenpress
yenpress.tumblr.com
instagram.com/yenpress

First Yen Press Edition: November 2017



Library of Congress Control Number: 2015952604

ISBNs: 978-0-316-44343-2 (paperback)
978-0-316-44655-6 (ebook)

10 9 8 7 6 5 4 3 2 1

BVG

Printed in the United States of America